Anonymous

Diary of an embassy from King George of Bohemia to King Louis XI of France in 1464

Anonymous

Diary of an embassy from King George of Bohemia to King Louis XI of France in 1464

ISBN/EAN: 9783337125745

Printed in Europe, USA, Canada, Australia, Japan

Cover: Foto ©ninafisch / pixelio.de

More available books at **www.hansebooks.com**

DIARY OF AN EMBASSY

FROM KING GEORGE OF BOHEMIA

TO KING LOUIS XI.

OF FRANCE

IN THE YEAR OF GRACE 1464.

FROM A CONTEMPORARY MANUSCRIPT, LITERALLY TRANSLATED

FROM THE ORIGINAL SLAVONIC

BY

A. H. WRATISLAW, M.A.,

HEAD MASTER OF THE GRAMMAR SCHOOL, BURY ST. EDMUND'S, AND FORMERLY
FELLOW AND TUTOR OF CHRIST'S COLLEGE,
CAMBRIDGE.

LONDON:
BELL AND DALDY, YORK STREET,
COVENT GARDEN.

1871.

CHISWICK PRESS:—PRINTED BY WHITTINGHAM AND WILKINS,
TOOKS COURT, CHANCERY LANE.

DIARY OF AN EMBASSY

FROM KING GEORGE OF BOHEMIA TO LOUIS XI. OF FRANCE, IN 1464.

INTRODUCTION.

GEORGE OF PODIEBRAD, King of Bohemia, who ascended the throne after a solemn election in 1458, was looked upon universally as the wisest statesman of his day in Europe. Still, all his wisdom and his many virtues were shipwrecked upon the one fact, that, as an Utraquist, he declined to render obedience to the Papal see in a point which it had itself conceded to the Bohemian Church, yet the renunciation of which it considered essential to its dignity and authority. King George endeavoured to bring about a council of crowned heads, in which the confusion then existing in Europe should be carefully considered, and means taken to introduce order and quiet into the empire, which was miserably tormented by warfare above and lawlessness beneath. It was also his design to lead the assembled princes to agree upon measures that should have the effect of restraining and regulating the action of the Roman Curia, which was endeavouring by every means to secure for itself the position of ultimate court of appeal in almost every question of importance. In the negotiations which he conducted for this purpose King George made great use of the services of the Chevalier Antoine Marini of Grenoble, who in March 1464 appeared at the Court of Mathias Corvinus, King of Hungary, as ambassador of the three kings, George of Bohemia, Casimir of Poland, and Louis XI. of France. Nothing daunted by partial failure with his son-in-law, the King of Hungary, who however finally consented to be represented, as well as King Casimir of Poland, by Antoine Marini at the Court of Louis XI., King George sent a solemn embassy on May 16, 1464 to the Court of France, at the head of which were Lord Albrecht Kostka of Postupitz, and the Chevalier Antoine Marini of Grenoble; their suite consisting of forty persons, mostly retainers of Albrecht Kostka.

The diary of the embassy was kept by one of the attachés named Jaroslaw, and was found in MS. by Dr. F. Palacky in the archives of the town of Budweis, in Bohemia.

INTRODUCTION.

Palacky made a careful copy of this, and laid it before the censorship of the press, with a request that he might be allowed to print it in the "*Czasopis*" or quarterly journal of the Bohemian Museum, which was then for the first time about to appear in the Bohemian language. His copy was returned to him with several passages struck out, which he was not allowed to print, they being considered disrespectful to the Church of Rome. Thus, this curious and interesting document was printed in 1827 with considerable gaps (*Censurlücken*); and when Dr. Palacky wished to obtain a fresh copy for his own use, he found that the manuscript itself had been spirited away out of the archives of Budweis, and no one knew what had become of it. It is feared that it has been destroyed, like many other documents, by some over-zealous and unscrupulous ecclesiastic.

INTRODUCTION.

As regards the translation, which is now laid before the British public, I made it from Palacky's printed transcript in July last at Prague, and went carefully over the more difficult passages with Pan Vrtatko, the Librarian of the National Museum, whom I beg to thank sincerely for his kind and valuable assistance.

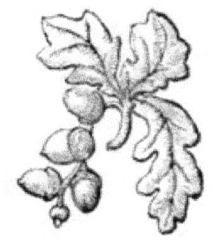

DIARY (DENNIK)
OF THE AMBASSADORS OF KING GEORGE,

SENT TO THE KING OF FRANCE, LOUIS XI., IN THE YEAR 1464.

FROM A CONTEMPORARY MS.

IN the year of God MCCCCLXIV. Departure of the Ambassadors of King George to the King of France and elsewhere. In the name of God may it prove prosperous!

On the Wednesday after St. Sophia (May 16) at 13 o'clock, we quitted Prague.

The first night we lay at Beraun, three miles from Prague.

The second at Pilsen, seven miles from Beraun.

The third at Tachow, six miles from Pilsen, at the house of Lord Burian. And there we were on Whit Sunday (20th May), and were honourably entertained by Lord Burian.

The fourth place at which we lay was Unsidl (Wunsiedel), a city belonging to the Margrave of Brandenburg, seven miles from Tachow. That day we breakfasted in the monastery of Waldsassy, four miles from Tachow, and were entertained by the monks. And about half a mile before we arrived at the monastery there met us a body of Germans, equipped like Turks, who were marching against the pagans. And when we came to Unsidl to lodge for the night, the Germans looked on us with unfriendly eyes. In Unsidl they keep the cannon-balls, which the Bohemians fired into the town, when they besieged it; and they keep these balls in the churchyard, and have fastened them to the church with chains, like relics.

Our fifth lodging, on Whitsun-Tuesday, was at Payrait (Baireuth), also a city belonging to the Margrave of Brandenburg, six miles from Unsidl. That day we breakfasted three miles from Unsidl, in a town belonging to the Margrave, named Fars (?); and we breakfasted in an inn, where a certain priest retails wine, beer, &c.; and he sold us everything per pound, and everything exceedingly dear—wine, beer, bread and hay, a pound of fish for five groschen, so that we paid two Hungarian florins for our breakfast. And when we arrived at Payrait, there too the Germans beheld us strangely; and a certain German wondered at us greatly and spake strangely.

Our sixth night's lodging on the Wednesday after Whitsunday was at Greifenberk (Gräfenberg), five miles from Payrait and four from Normberk (Nüremberg). This town is fairly well fortified, and belongs to the Bohemian crown. Two citizens of Normberk hold it, and have received it as a fief from the king of Bohemia. That day we breakfasted on the road three miles from Payrait, in a town named Pegnitz, under a castle named Pehmstein; and here we left behind a horse, a good one, belonging to Lord John Czervikosky.

Our seventh night-quarters were in Normberk on the Thursday before St. Urban. Here we were welcomed by the lords of Normberk, and presented with twenty pitchers of Italian, French, and other wine.

On the morrow, St. Urban's Day, (May 25th), there went with us a citizen, one of the senators, and afterwards two, showing us the town, and they also took us to the castle. That day some of us saw great irregularity, particularly this, that a priest went from the King a good way into a street with the body of God, and no one followed him. And there rode a German through the same street a very little before the priest, calling himself Urban, and after him went a great multitude of people, old and young, men and women, bearing banners: and did any one look back or kneel? Not one! But where wine was retailed they drank, and drink was given them in abundance.

On the morrow, Saturday, they showed us the relics, the spear of God, a piece of the Holy Cross, the chains of St. Peter, St. Paul, and St. John Baptist, a piece of the manger at Bethlehem, a tooth of St. John the Evangelist, a piece of his shirt, a piece of the arm of St. Anne, the mother of the Virgin Mary, the sword of St. Maurice, which an angel brought him from heaven, the crown of Charlemagne, and his sword, which an angel also brought him from heaven, if it is but as they say. Gauntlets and armour for the arms and legs, and many other curious things we saw, which I could not catalogue here, neither did it seem good to me to do so.

On the morrow, being Trinity Sunday, we left Normberk and went five miles to Onspach (Ansbach), where Prince Albert, Margrave of Brandenburg, has his court. Lord Albert Kostka was upset, as he sat in his carriage with Lord Antony, and strangely did Lord Antony cry out. And when we arrived at Onspach, the Margrave did not allow our coachmen to cook anything in the inns, but we went to table in the castle with the Margrave, and were very honourably entertained. We were there the next day (Monday), and Lord Albert and Lord Antony rode hunting with the Margrave. And that day the Margrave took us to the Princess in her drawing-room, where not everybody goes.

On the morrow (Tuesday), the Margrave sent with us two of his courtiers, who accompanied and escorted us to Wirtemburk, to the Count of Wirtemburk; and if we had not had them with us, we should have been in great difficulties. In Onspach we left behind two grooms, who had fallen sick. That day, the Tuesday after Trinity Sunday, we travelled five miles from Onspach to the city of Tynklspihl (Dünkelsbühl), which is a tolerably handsome city, and they told us it was an imperial one.

On the morrow, Wednesday, we travelled six miles to a city called Swewiskmund,

(Gmünd), which is a tolerably handsome city. We went to this city through a certain stream a mile from the town, and on the morrow we crossed it two miles on the other side of the town, and they told us that we must cross it 141 times.

On the morrow, Thursday, being Corpus Christi day (May 31), we went five miles to a city named Stokard (Stuttgart), which belongs to the Counts of Wirtemburk, where these counts reside and have their court; and here we were honourably welcomed by their council. On the road we breakfasted in a city called Shorndorf in a very well-furnished inn; and we passed through a city called Kenshtot (Canstadt), only half a mile from Stokard. When we arrived at the city of Stokard, many beautiful damsels and ladies sent to us to come to them; and others came themselves with purses, girdles, &c., that we might make purchases; so that Lord Bavor lamented that he had ever married. Thence we were accompanied by these Counts to the city of Fortz.

On the morrow, being the Friday after Corpus Christi, we travelled four very long miles from Stokard to a city belonging to the Counts of Paden, named Fortz (? Pforzheim). Here we remained the next day, Saturday, being St. Marcellus's day (June 2), and stayed in an inn, which was kept by a very fat and coquettish hostess. Two miles on the road we drank good water on a hill, under a castle called Waisach.

On the morrow, being Sunday, the Octave of the Holy Trinity, we travelled five miles to the city of Paden (Baden), where the Margrave of Paden resides and has his court. Here we received an honourable welcome from the Margrave's council; and they sent us from the castle a good large cask of wine on a cart, and some venison. And on the morrow, Monday, we were invited to dinner with the Margrave in the castle, and were greatly honoured by the Margrave and the Emperor's sister, the Margravine. And we bathed in warm baths, some of us with countesses; and in the dance we knelt when the bell was rung for the Pater noster, each kneeling with his partner.

On the morrow, Monday, we quitted Paden and the Margrave, and travelled five miles to Straspurk (Strasburg), the Margrave giving us an escort to this city. Further than this he could not ensure our safety, but sent a letter by his servants to the lords of Straspurk, to do so for the sake of the King of Bohemia, our gracious lord, and on his account also for the sake of the Margrave; and if we had need of or required them in aught, to counsel and aid us. And those proud lords, the citizens of Straspurk, came to us in the inn, and welcomed us honourably, and gave us fish and wine, and inquired after the health of the King of Bohemia, our gracious lord. And when Lord Albert Kostka spake with them and inquired which way we could travel safely into France, they told us, that we could not travel safely at all, which ever way we turned; but that, whether we went down the Rhine to Kolin (Cologne), or went up the Rhine, we should undoubtedly have a fight. So they told us, that, if we wished and it was agreeable to us, they would give us fifty or one hundred horsemen, to escort us through these dangerous passages to France or whithersoever we would. And thus it came to pass, that they gave us fifty well-armed horsemen on good horses, queer-looking Germans, twenty-eight of whom were lancers. And in particular they warned us against a certain Count, named Graf Hanus von Ebersburg, that we should beware of him; with regard to whom we ascertained on our return at Constance, that he undoubtedly waited for us on the mountains, but, because we were on our guard, durst not do anything to us. Moreover as to how this Count came to us in our inn at Strasburk, and what he said to Lord Albert Kostka, all treacherously, much might be written, but I have not had leisure to write it all.

On the morrow, very early, soon after midnight, we went from Strasburk, following the course of the Rhine upwards, till we came to a tolerably good city named Slitstot (Schlittstadt) which they say is also an imperial town. It lies amongst marshes, six miles from Strasburk, and here we breakfasted. We went that day two miles further under mountains to a town named Villa, belonging to the people of Strasburk. Here we were told again, that we should certainly not cross the mountains and forests of the frontiers without a considerable skirmish and battle. So the fifty horsemen, that we had from Strasburk, engaged at their own cost fifty footmen of this town belonging to the people of Strasburk. Thus we had in all, escorting us over the mountains, one hundred well-armed Germans, and were also thoroughly on our guard ourselves. And Lord Antony wrote a letter in French, and sent it to the chief officer of the Prince of Lorraine, requesting an escort through the Principality. So it came to pass, that the chief officer sent fifty footmen to meet us close to the frontiers, as far as the Principality of Lorraine extends into the mountains.

On the morrow, Thursday, we travelled

four miles by a very bad road over infernal mountains to the city of Sandii (St. Diez), which lies in the territory of the Prince of Lorraine. This territory and Prince appertain to the Crown of the kingdom of France, and it is called Loturingia (Lorraine); and we were told, that the Prince is the son of the King of Sicily and has his palaces here on the frontiers.

On the morrow, Friday, we travelled five short miles, which in those lands and regions are called leagues (leuky), to the town of Rayun (Raon); and we were still accompanied by an escort from the town of Sandii. The chief officer of the Prince of Lorraine, who had sent the fifty footmen to meet us, escorted us himself to a town, which is called Lenshtot (Luneville).

On the morrow, Saturday, we travelled seven long leagues to a large village, named

Villa S. Nicolai, the "village of St. Nicholas," which others call Portus S. Nicolai, the "haven of St. Nicholas." It is a large place, they say that there are 300 householders in it. The Prince of Lorraine holds it; and it is said, that he does not allow the French in the village to fortify themselves for fear of their taking part against him. We breakfasted in the town of Lenshtot, two leagues from the village.

On the morrow, Sunday, they showed us in the village the hand of St. Nicholas[1] and other relics. In the church of St. Nicholas lies such a quantity of iron, fetters, chains, &c., that every one of us, who was present, declared that he had never seen a greater quantity of such iron; and without deception, I think that it could not be carried off in

---

[1] In Bohemian "Mikulas."

fifty waggons. That day, Sunday, after breakfast, we travelled six leagues, to a city called Taul (Toul), which is said to be an imperial town. There is a bishopric in it, and the bishop is a young man, the son of the Marshal of the Duke of Burgundy. And we marvelled greatly in this town.

On the morrow, Monday, we travelled seven leagues to a city called Barluduk (Bar-le-duc), where the King of Sicily[1] resides, and has his court. And Lord Albert was overturned with Lord Antony, and the unfortunate coachman was killed, and there was no help for it. We breakfasted on the road in a certain village, a mile from the town of Barluduk, and here we found a monk in company with a pretty damsel, who travelled with us and performed the service of the

---

[1] René, of the House of Anjou.

mass. And straightway there came out to meet us the council of the King of Sicily, and welcomed us honourably. On the morrow, the Wednesday before St. Vitus, at vesper-time, an audience was granted us in the presence of the King of Sicily. Here first Lord Albert Kostka presented a salutation from the King of Bohemia, and delivered letters credential; and when the letters credential had been read, straightway the King took Lord Albert as well as Lord Antony into his chamber with his council. And there they were a good long time, till they had an answer from the King, all this being in secret council.

On the morrow, Thursday, Lord Albert invited the privy council of the King of Sicily to dinner, and the King invited us all to supper, where we were honourably entertained. Afterwards the officers of the King reimbursed us all that we had paid during those days in the inns.

On the morrow, St. Vitus's day (June 15), we travelled seven leagues to a village named Shumitz (?), which lies in a district called Kampania (Champagne). The country is well enough in appearance, but has no water and very few forests and villages. The soil is chalky, and the houses, churches, and all kinds of walls are all of clunch.

On the morrow, Saturday, we travelled fifteen leagues over a very level plain through this county of Kampania. And we came to a city, called in French Reims, and in Latin Remis, a good large city; Lord Antony said it was as large as Prague, but I could not agree thereto. Therein is a fine and handsome church of the Mother of God, in which the King of France is anointed king, and in the church of St. Dionysius about a Bohemian mile from Paris he is invested with the majesty and robes of St. Charles, and then, and not till then, is he crowned in Paris. It was likewise near the city of Remis, that St. Dionysius was beheaded, at a distance from the town twice or thrice as great as that from Prague to the gallows belonging to Prague. They say that after his head was cut off St. Dionysius took his head and carried it to this church of the Mother of God, where he was finally buried.

On the morrow, Sunday, we travelled eleven leagues from this city to a village called Villa Beatæ Virginis, " the village of the Mother of God," (Notre Dame de Liesse?). And we crossed a stream called Sána, five miles from Remis; and this river runs to Paris.[1] Further on we passed a handsome

---

[1] Here Palacky remarks that the writer has made a

city called Lan (Laon). There is a very celebrated pilgrimage to the Village of the Mother of God, where we lay; and here they cheat the people out of money in an extraordinary manner.

On the morrow, Monday, we travelled twelve leagues to a city called Villa S. Quintini, the "Village of St. Kwintin," (St. Quentin). And, straightway, that day we bathed in a bath [1] . . . . and some of our people had themselves shaved, just as in Sodom.

On the morrow, Tuesday, we travelled

---

trip. The river was certainly not the Sána (Seine, which runs to Paris, but the Asna (Aisne), which joins the Oise at the town of Compiègne and runs into the Seine some miles below Paris.

[1] This is one of the hiatuses due to the Austrian Censure of the Press. It is not easy to conjecture what is omitted, or to explain the fragment, that has been allowed to remain.

nine leagues to a good large village named Lihons.

On the morrow, Wednesday, we travelled nine leagues to a good large city, named Amiens; and passed through a city called Korbel (Corbie), four leagues from Amiens. Here in Amiens on the morrow, Thursday, we saw the King of Cyprus, in Latin *Rex Cypri*. Here first we were told correctly where the King of France was. For previously no one had been able to tell us for certain, and that because he was never long in one place, but was always roaming about on the chase and hunting. In this town of Amiens is a fine church, where they have many relics, the head of St. John Baptist, &c.

On the morrow, being the Friday before St. John Baptist, Lord Antony went with his servants, and with Jaroslaw, to a town called Sampo (St. Pol), in Latin *Villa S. Pauli*, the "village of St. Paul;" which is a good deal smaller than Czesky Brod (Böhmisch Brod). There is a castle in it. They told us that this town belonged to the Duke of Burgundy, and we also saw him there, a grey-haired old man.[1] On the road we breakfasted at a city called Turlan (Dourlens), which is a tolerably handsome town; it may be half-way between Amiens and Sampo. Here, when Lord Antony found the King, he entreated and prayed His Royal Grace, that His Royal Grace would please to appoint and ordain, when and where he would please to hear us on our embassy. Hereupon His Majesty beheld us very favourably and gladly, and commanded that we should go to a city named Abbevilla, in Latin *Abbatis Villa,* "Abbot's village," a tolerably hand-

---

[1] Philip the Good, father of Charles the Rash.

some town; in other respects as large as Amiens, but it is not half filled with houses, but there are orchards and gardens in it. And through it runs a good large river, and up this river come large ships from the sea, bringing curious fish and sea-creatures. And so His Royal Grace told us to go on before him, because he intended to follow us on Monday or Tuesday, or at latest, on Wednesday to this city of Abbeville.

On the morrow, Saturday, we went back from the King to Lord Albert, at the city of Amiens; and here Lord Antony told Lord Albert what the King's Majesty had commanded.

On the morrow, Sunday, the day of St. John, the Divine Baptist, we travelled seven leagues to the city of Abbeville, whither His Royal Majesty commanded us to go. And, when we arrived there, the silly people marvelled at us above measure. The King had said that on Monday or Tuesday, or, at latest, on Wednesday, he would follow us to the town of Abbeville, and that he would immediately give us an audience there. He did not come then, but after some days approached nearer to the city of Abbeville; so that he was only five leagues therefrom, in a certain village named Dumpir (Dompierre), in which there is a castle in the midst of marshes. Here was the King, and with him the Queen also; for, when we came to the city of Abbeville, the Queen was there with her brother, the King of Cyprus; and on the morrow, the Monday after St. John, she went forthwith to the village with the king, her brother. Then, when the King did not come either on Tuesday or Wednesday, as he had told us, Lord Antony went with only two others to His Majesty. Then His

Majesty, at the instance of Lord Antony, commanded that we should come to His Majesty in the castle of Dumpir, on the Saturday after SS. Peter and Paul. Meanwhile, on the Thursday before SS. Peter and Paul, Lord Albert Kostka had invited to dinner the council of the Duke of Milan, and some of the authorities of the city of Abbeville; and these people marvelled greatly that the Bohemians conducted themselves so handsomely and properly at meals, &c.[1]

Then on the Saturday after St. Peter

---

[1] People at that day seem to have obtained their ideas of the Bohemians from such descriptions as that given by Æneas Sylvius of the Taborites:—"These men were quite black from constant exposure to the sun and wind, as well as to the smoke of the camp. Their appearance was horrid and terrible, their eyes were those of an eagle, their hair bristled, their beards long, their bodies covered with hair, and their skin so hard, that it appeared capable of resisting iron, as much as a cuirass."

(June 30) we went in the morning early to the King in the village of Dumpir. And when we had gone four leagues from Abbeville to a village named Krs (Crecy?), only a league from Dumpir, where the King was hunting, we breakfasted; and Lord Antony went thence with two others to the King, to ascertain at what hour we might have access to His Majesty. Then he came back to us, it might be perhaps four hours from mid-day, which in Prague would be twenty o'clock; whereupon we went immediately to the King. And when we came to the village where the King was, a certain distinguished lord and other knights of the land of France rode out to meet us and welcomed us; and this gentleman conducted us to his own lodging or a place in front of his lodging. Here, dismounting from our horses in front of the lodging, we went forthwith with this lord into the castle to the King. When we were admitted into the castle, we stood a good long while before the King's chamber, before we were admitted into his presence. When we were admitted into the presence of His Majesty, Lord Albert Kostka first pronounced a formal salutation from the King of Bohemia, and forthwith delivered the letter credential from the self-same King of Bohemia. Then Lord Antony likewise pronounced a salutation from the Kings of Hungary and Poland, and forthwith delivered letters credential from both Kings. Then the King himself read the letters credential to his council, but he read that of the King of Bohemia first. And when he had read them all through, he bade Lord Kostka and Lord Antony take their places upon a seat prepared for the purpose. They declined, and refused to sit down, till the King's council said, that it was customary for royal ambassadors to perform their embassy sitting. And before they took their seats two members of the council, coming up to Lord Kostka and Lord Antony, told them from the King, that His Majesty wished us to perform our embassy as briefly as possible and to speak briefly. Then Lord Kostka said, that he would speak briefly, and so they sat down and spoke. First, Lord Albert Kostka spoke in Latin, excusing himself and saying, that he had rather perform the duties of a knight than speak in presence of so mighty and Most Christian King; and thus he spoke long and much, all which I could not write down here word for word. But, briefly, the end and intent of all this speech was this: that the King of Bohemia entreated and prayed the King of France, as the Most Christian King, and one who loved the common good of the Christian faith, that His Majesty would be pleased to bring to pass a parliament and convocation of Christian kings and princes, to meet in person or by their plenipotentiaries in one place and at one time, where and when the King of France should appoint and ordain; and that the King of Bohemia desired this for the glory of God and the exaltation of the Christian Faith and of the Holy Roman Catholic Church, and for the Holy Christian Empire, &c. And this he expressed at good breadth and length, so that it took about an hour or more. Likewise also Lord Antony spoke on the same matter, in Latin from the King of Poland and in French from the King of Hungary, although he said from both Kings more than Lord Kostka had expressed from the King of Bohemia. For he spoke, recounting what had happened to him at the court of the

King of Hungary, how some bishops had wished to excommunicate him, and what he had heard there concerning the King of France, how the Pope had written letters reviling his Majesty; likewise also concerning the adventures, which he had met with at the court of the King of Poland; and likewise he related what had happened to him, when he went from the King of France to the Venetian lords; and how lovingly disposed the King of Bohemia, the King of Poland, and the King of Hungary were towards the King of France, and how greatly their subjects loved the King of France and the land of France; and especially that the Bohemian lords were very well inclined towards the King and Kingdom of France, and so likewise were the Venetian lords. And all this he expressed very fully in Latin and in French.

Thereto the King of France commanded answer to be made through his chancellor, that this matter and desire of the King of Bohemia, which Lord Albert Kostka had stated, was a great matter, and that it was not meet to give an answer thereto so soon, but with good consideration. So he commanded, that we should go back again to Abbeville, and promised that the King would follow us on Tuesday, or at latest on Wednesday, forthwith, and that then he would make an end and settlement for us concerning all matters. So we returned forthwith the same day, Saturday, to the city of Abbeville, and arrived there in the evening.

Afterwards, on the Monday, Tuesday, and Wednesday, when the royal council, the Bishop of Evreux,[1] the Lord Chancellor and

---

[1] Jean de la Balue.

other lords appertaining to the council, came after us before the King to the town, they sent for Lord Antony and had a curious dispute with him, as he said, particularly with regard to the meeting or parliament of all kings and princes, and also other matters. And they bade him speak with Lord Albert about showing their letters, in Latin *literas commissarias*, in Bohemian " letters of power or commission," and asked: " What powers (in Latin *libertatem*) have ye?" &c. Then Lord Albert Kostka long refused to do this, and that in order to show his powers and letters to the King himself. But when Lord Antony diligently persisted in his request, and said, that the King had given them orders to that effect, that they, that is to say, the bishops and the Lord Chancellor with the rest of the council, should ascertain from us, what letters of commission or powers we had to negotiate or conclude anything: then Lord Albert consented to go to them himself with the documents. But Lord Antony said, that they had bidden him to come by himself without Lord Albert Kostka; and also, that they would not say that before Lord Kostka, which they had to say to Lord Antony.[1] All this Lord Antony said to Lord Kostka; and further Lord Antony said, that such was the custom of Louis, the present King of France; and thus he continually endeavoured to persuade Lord Albert, so that he gave him the letters of commission. Lord Antony took the letters and carried them to the Lord Chancellor in the inn. And when the bishops with the rest of the council inspected the letters, again they had another dispute

---

[1] Lord Antony was a Catholic, Lord Kostka was a moderate Utraquist with Catholic tendency.

with Lord Antony, saying, that we had no other commission and powers given us by letter from the King of Bohemia, save to confirm and complete the friendship and good relations, which had subsisted between the kingdoms and Kings of France and Bohemia. And in reply thereto Lord Antony admitted that it was so, and said that at this time of the present embassy we required no longer documentary commission, save only to complete those negotiations. Some days afterwards, still before the arrival of the King, Lord Albert and Lord Antony were sent for together by the Lord Chancellor, the Patriarch of Jerusalem, and the Bishop of Evreux, to come together to them in the lodging of the Lord Chancellor. They went there and had there an extraordinary conversation with them, no one being allowed to enter the room with them, save only those two. But we,

Ruprecht, Wenceslas Strachota, and Jaroslaw, listened at a certain window, how they were exclaiming against one another and were having an extraordinary dispute, especially respecting the parliament or meeting of kings and princes, saying, that the King of Bohemia ought not to desire this, especially without the consent of the Holy Father, the Pope, and the Christian Emperor; and that it would appertain best to the Holy Father to negotiate this with the Emperor; and that the King of Bohemia ought not to interfere in the matter. Likewise with regard to the formation of friendly relations between the Kings of Bohemia and France, that it ought not be without the knowledge of the Holy Father. Many other insulting and unprofitable speeches were made, especially by the Patriarch, the Chancellor and a certain Magister, all of which I could not write nor even remember. To their speeches Lord Antony began to reply first in an earnest and high-pitched voice, saying:[1] " . . . . you always want nothing good to be negotiated without the Pope." And many other things did he say in great anger. And Lord Albert also said: " We reserve all things that appertain to the Holy Father for His Holiness, and likewise for His Imperial Majesty; but it is a marvellous thing, that you prelates are displeased at seeing secular people, or endeavour to prevent them from, effecting anything good by negotiation together, but want every thing to pass through the prelatical power and office, and require that you clergy should know every thing about all secular affairs." And he also said a good deal be-

---

[1] Here is another of these shameful " Censure gaps," " *Censur Lücken*," as Palacký calls them in his history.

sides touching the point, that who will can make friends with whom he will without the permission of the Holy Father, &c. And this he said, because they had stated, that it was not proper for the King of France to enter into friendly relations with the King of Bohemia, because the latter was under the papal ban; and also that letters had been written from Bohemia after us, describing the King of Bohemia and Her Majesty the Queen and all of us members of the embassy as all heretics, and containing many other dishonourable things; for instance, the council of the King of France told us what people had written from Bohemia after us, striving with all diligence to prevent the King of France from concluding anything with us respecting the matters about which we were sent, and that because we were all heretics, which was very painful to hear. And, dear Lord God, be pleased to make them known, and be pleased to reveal them, that they may no more strive for the evil and dishonour of the kingdom of Bohemia!

Afterwards on the Tuesday before St. Margaret (July 10), the King followed us to the city of Abbeville, but never did what he had promised us. For he had told us, that he would follow us on the Tuesday, or at latest on the Wednesday, but did not come till that day; and likewise he said, that he would complete our business in six days, and that His Majesty would not leave the city of Abbeville, till he had completed our business. But none of this came to pass. But on the morrow, Wednesday, Lord Antony went to His Royal Grace, and entreated His Majesty to be so good as to dispatch us back to Bohemia. And His Majesty commanded Lord Antony, that he should go with His

Majesty to a city called Diepa (Dieppe), twenty leagues from Abbeville. It is a tolerably handsome city, lying along the sea on the seashore, but the air in it is very unhealthy from the putrefaction of the fish; for many seafish are sold in it, and large heaps of them lie and putrefy. They also manufacture salt in the neighbourhood.

On Friday, St. Margaret's day, we went with the King to this city of Diepa, and arrived before the King. For the King slept in a certain town named Sentrin, two leagues from the town of Eou (Eu), where we could not obtain any bread; such great abundance was there! Here commences the district of Normandia. In the evening, it might be perhaps an hour to night, the King followed us to the city of Diepa with a very small suite.

On the morrow, Saturday, the King went to a certain castle, two leagues from the city of Diepa, named Akar; it is situated on a slope and is neither strong nor handsome. Here the Bishops and Chancellor told us to follow the King to the castle; but Lord Albert was angered and would not go.

On the morrow, Sunday (July 15), the King went a league beyond the castle to a very inferior castle, named Novilla, belonging to a certain citizen of Diepa. It lies beside a stream, which runs to the city of Diepa, and is quite by itself. That day, Sunday, the King sent for us to come to His Majesty, and we went after dinner three leagues to the castle. Here Lord Albert spoke with the King, but none of us were there, save only Lord Antony and the rest of the council. That day, Lord Albert was made a member of the King's council, and received a letter-patent to the effect, that he was to enjoy all profits and all dignities, even as the chiefest councillor of His Majesty did; and hereupon he forthwith took the oath to the King. And Lord Albert obtained a second letter patent for the Prince Bishop of Wratislaw (Breslau), Lord Jost, and took on his behalf the oath on being admitted a member of the council; but he will have to take the oath himself, when the council of the King of France comes to Bohemia after All Saints. Then forthwith the King commanded the Patriarch of Jerusalem and the Bishop of Evreux, the Lord Chancellor, and the rest of the council then present with His Majesty, to complete and write the letters, which they had to complete, without delay, even as the first letters of these engagements and friendly relations between the kings and kingdoms of France and Bohemia had been. And Lord Antony said, that the King spoke in the council to those bishops and the rest, saying: " Whether any one like it or mislike it, I will be on good terms with the King of Bohemia, and will enter into goodwill and friendship with him." And forthwith he commanded his council to complete the letters. Immediately thereupon Lord Albert took leave of the King, and we went back that day (Sunday) to the city of Diepa.

On the morrow, Monday, the bishops and the rest of the council exhibited to Lord Albert and Lord Antony a document containing and comprehending the engagements and friendly relations of the Kings and kingdoms of France and Bohemia, to see how it pleased them. When they had inspected the writings thus put together, the document forthwith displeased them in many respects; so they deferred it to the Tuesday, that they might all meet about it, the bishops and the rest of the council.

On the morrow, Tuesday, they met together in the lodging of the Patriarch of Jerusalem, and the Patriarch of Jerusalem began to speak, saying, that what that letter, which had been shown us, exhibited and contained, was sufficient. Lord Albert would not in any wise agree thereto; and that, because this document contained and expressly mentioned, that these engagements and friendly relations were not to be to the prejudice of the Duke of Burgundy, especially in that which might concern the land of Luxemburg; stating and setting forth at length, how the father of Louis the present King of France purchased the land of Luxemburg from the Queen of Poland for 60,000 florins; and that Louis the present King of France had granted it to the Duke of Burgundy, as his father's chosen and dearest friend. These things the Patriarch explained at great length and in great detail. Thereto Lord Albert briefly replied, saying: "We have not been sent about these matters, that we ought to deal with them now; but, my lord Prelates, be so good as to know, that the Queen of Poland had no right to sell the land of Luxemburg. For King Ladislaw was not the legal heir, neither was the Queen of Poland, his sister, the heiress of the land of Bohemia: but King Ladislaw of glorious memory was elected and accepted as King into Bohemia. If then the Duke of Burgundy should exhibit or possess any right, the King of Bohemia might well be provided with 60,000 florins, if he wished to have the land of Luxemburg again; but the Queen of Poland could not in any wise sell the land of Luxemburg in inheritance. If then the Duke of Burgundy proves this, why should he not have the benefit of it? We have not been sent about this matter now, neither will we treat of anything concerning that land. We are not endeavouring to take it away from the Duke of Burgundy, neither will we through these engagements and friendly relations absolutely sever it from the land of Bohemia: for we know that the land of Luxemburg was granted and assigned by a King of France of glorious memory, for an everlasting possession and for ever to the Kingdom of Bohemia. And if the King of Bohemia, our gracious lord, shall desire to have it again, let him endeavour to obtain it; we are not sent about this matter on this embassy." And many other things were said about the land of Luxemburg, which I have not been able to remember or write. Likewise they spoke very earnestly about this, if we wished the letters to be written and concluded, that it should not stand written *in literâ commissariâ*, in the letter of commission from our King, "*wěwoda Lucemburský;*"[1] but as the old letters were, copies of which they had with them: and because the King of France wished it so to be done, as the counterparts of the old protocols exhibit. Thereto we willingly consented.

On the morrow, Wednesday (July 18), we wrote a new *literam commissariam*, a letter of commission, and gave it them forthwith the same day. And when the Patriarch of Jerusalem and the Bishop of Evreux inspected the letter, again it pleased them not; for there was written in it: "George, by the grace of God, King of Bohemia, Margrave of Moravia, Duke of Silesia, and Margrave of Lusatia, &c.;" but they wished only one title to stand, thus: "George, by

---

[1] Duke of Luxemburg.

the grace of God, King of Bohemia, &c." They said, that the King of France, in giving his council their commission to compose a letter in his behalf, thought fit to describe himself by only one title, thus : " Louis, by the grace of God, King of France, &c." Thus, on the morrow (Thursday), we were again obliged to write another letter, as the old letters exhibit, to please them; and to this we agreed, and wrote it, and brought it, and showed it to them again. When the Bishops had inspected it, they accepted it. And when they had accepted it, we desired them to lend us the principal protocol of these engagements, that we might write a principal protocol, and give it them on behalf of the King of Bohemia; and they might also give us one from their King, the King of France. Then the Patriarch of Jerusalem and the secretary Rolant gave us the document, which they had shown us first, and to which we had previously refused to consent; and Rolant, the lord secretary of the King of France, told us, that he had already written and sealed a principal protocol in accordance with that document. Then we again absolutely refused to consent thereto, saying, that we should have to return to Bohemia without the letters and without any agreement; and that, had we known this, and had not the King of France given us assurance by his letters, we should not have travelled a foot from the kingdom of Bohemia, about the friendly relations and confirmation of the engagements; and that the King of France had as much need of them as the King of Bohemia; and a good deal of other tolerably high language did we use towards them, so that they gave us no other answer thereto, than that, if we wanted to have that document differently, especially in the point above mentioned respecting the land of Luxemburg, we should go about it to the King ourselves, and speak about it to His Majesty ourselves; but that without the knowledge of His Majesty they neither durst nor could alter the document. Thereto we agreed, and wanted to go to the King forthwith. They consulted, and told us not to go, for they would go themselves, and that Lord Antony alone should go with them. So it came to pass, that the Patriarch of Jerusalem went, and the Bishop of Evreux, and our Lord Antony with them. And when they came back from the King, Lord Antony told us, that the King's Majesty commanded, that the business was to be settled with us according to our wish; and whatsoever protocol of high contract and friendly relations we made for them from our King, they were to make us just such another in all respects from their King. And so it was done, though with great labour on our part. For the Lord Chancellor of the King of France was in one town with the seal, and the Secretary, who had to write the letters, was elsewhere; till it could not but fall, and did fall upon us, that, after giving them the letters from our King, we wrote ourselves those from the King of France, and the Lord Chancellor with the Lord Secretary and the rest of the council took the oath and sealed them; and that not till afterwards, in the city of Rotomag (Rouen). Thus we were detained in the city of Diepa till Sunday, owing to their extraordinary jugglery.

On Sunday, St. Mary Magdalene's day (July 22), the King again went from that castle elsewhere, in the direction of the city of Ruan (Rouen), in Latin *Rotomagus*, and was somewhere only two miles from the city of Ruan. We travelled that day fourteen leagues from the city of Diepa to that of Ruan; and that day we breakfasted in a certain tavern, and here were stolen the letters given by the King of Bohemia to Hanus Causar, constituting him a herald. And not far from this city of Ruan, a monk upset himself,[1] . . . . as he sat in the carriage, upon Lord Antony; and Lord Albert cursed him in an extraordinary manner, and especially because Lord Bavor had knelt down.

On the morrow we took leave of Lord Antony, and separated; leaving here Wenceslas Strachota and Leonard, for Lord Albert

---

[1] Here comes another of those gaps, which do such honour to the Austrian Censorship of the Press. An amusing scene appears to be lost.

would not leave Jaroslaw, to wait for the Lord Chancellor and the Secretary to complete and seal the letters, which were already written. We ourselves travelled that day (Monday), twelve good long leagues, from Ruan to a village named Villa St. Clarii, the village of St. Claria (St. Clair).

On the morrow, Tuesday, we travelled thirteen leagues towards Paris, and lay that night in the city of St. Dionysius (St. Denis). On the road we breakfasted in a city named Pontors (Pontoise), under which runs a river called the Ors (Oise). Here first we entered the true France, as we returned; for we had previously left it on the left hand on our way to the King. In Pontors there was a battle between the French and Swiss.

On the morrow, Wednesday, St. James's day, in the morning at mass in the church of St. Dionysius they showed us a very large number of relics, which I could not describe, but only marvel at, neither could I remember them, they are so numerous, and of very precious jewels, the crown of the King of France, two golden crucifixes, like boys seven years old, both of pure gold, so the priests there said, and very many other jewels. And they keep them very badly.

The day after St. James's day we travelled three very short leagues, as it were a good Bohemian mile, to Paris. We were in Paris the next day, Thursday, and went on to the towers in the church of the Mother of God, in French Notredama, the most celebrated church in Paris; and from these towers we marvelled at the width, length and magnitude of the city of Paris, for from them all Paris can be seen.

On the morrow, Friday, we went to the monasteries beyond Paris; and meanwhile arrived Wenceslas Strachota and Leonard, bringing the letters for which we were waiting.

On the morrow, Saturday, we equipped a courier on horseback to go to the King's Majesty in Bohemia, writing to His Majesty that we should return to Bohemia by Italy, and how it had gone with us. That day, Saturday, we travelled fourteen leagues in the direction of the land of Italy to a village named Tampls (Estampes?).

On the morrow we travelled twenty leagues to the city of Orliens, in Latin Aurelianensis (Orleans), which district is a principality, and in the city is a bishopric, and under it flows a good large river, over which is a long bridge. Near it were slain 16,000 English, whom a certain maiden, Joan, defeated: so the French told us.

On the morrow, Monday, we travelled

eleven leagues to the village of Perfitte (Pierrefitte), in Latin Petraficta.

On the morrow, Tuesday, we travelled eleven leagues to the city of Burges (Bourges), in Latin Burgensis civitas; it is a principality, and is now held by the brother of the present King of France, Prince Charles. Here we saw a handsome house; they said that the work of this house is worth 100,000 florins, and one stone in a room is worth 1000 florins; it is gilt. In this house we saw a great dragon of leather, of the shape of a lizard, but very large. Here we engaged three Frenchmen to make tapestry and carpets in Bohemia, but afterwards they all ran away.

On the morrow, Wednesday, we went seven leagues to a village named Dunlaroy (Dun-le-roi), in Latin Da Regi; it is a tolerably large village.

On the morrow, Thursday, we travelled

eleven leagues to the city of Borbon (Bourbon), in which there is a warm bath. Here we also bathed in the warm bath, and had extraordinary bathing-dresses.[1] This district is a principality, and is called the Principality of Borbon.

On the morrow, Friday, we travelled five leagues from this warm bath to the city of Molinis (Moulins), and here is the court of the Prince of Borbon. It is a tolerably handsome town, and there is a castle in it. The Prince says that he has to wife a daughter of the King of France, so the French in the town told us: I don't then know what sort of daughter . . . .[2]

On the morrow, Saturday, we travelled

---

[1] Literally "girt ourselves in an extraordinary manner."

[2] Another gap due to the Austrian censor, who has evidently, for some reason or other, suppressed a pretty piece of scandal of the day.

seven leagues to a fortified town, named Palisa (La Palisse).

On the morrow,[1] Monday (Aug. 6), we travelled eight good Bohemian miles to the city of Lyon, in Latin Lugdonia. Here we were Wednesday and Thursday,[1] and there was at the time the annual fair in the city, and a great multitude of merchants from Normberk (Nürnberg), and elsewhere. These merchants and a certain Magister, a German, advised Lord Albert not to go by Mediolan (Milan) and Italy over the mountains, saying, that he had a nearer and that a safe way to Bohemia, and that he could go with a carriage travelling by Constance and Ulm. And they said it was only seventy miles from the city of Lyon, where the fair was, to

---

[1] There appears to be a little confusion here, days being omitted.

Constance. Lord Albert, thinking, perhaps, that they would be as short miles as in France, would not cross the mountains without a carriage, but wished to have a carriage with him, because he could not always travel on horseback. So he sent two grooms and Jaroslaw, and they engaged a certain guide, Pidrman (Biederman), who knew neither the road nor how to speak. And we travelled with the carriage on Friday, the day of St. Wawrinetz (Laurence), to a town named Burgurd, seven leagues from Lyon. But Lord Albert with his suite followed us on Saturday on horseback by another road over the mountains as far as the imperial city of Geneva. And Wenceslas Strachota likewise on Saturday went from Lyon into Italy to study with a canon from the grave of St. James.

On the morrow, Saturday, we travelled

with the carriage ten leagues to a fortified town named Releky, and breakfasted in a town named Jenensis (Yene?). That day too we crossed the river Rodanus (Rhone) with great danger. Here we entered into the country or district of Savoy, in Latin Sabaudia; it is an exceedingly mountainous district.

On the morrow, Sunday, we travelled four leagues after mass and after breakfasting to a fortified town named Seseli (Seyssel), where the Duke of Savoy resides, and has his court. The town is built on both sides of the Rhone in the midst of mountains; and there is a bridge over the river Rhone. That day we travelled by an infernal—not road—but by rocks and mountains, where few or no good[1] people have travelled with

---

[1] The inference intended appears to be, that, though no *good* people ever did so, yet people in league with the devil might have managed it.

such a carriage as we did. Having no road we were obliged to take the carriage to pieces, and convey it on the Rhone up stream about a Bohemian mile. And here we were weary of our lives, or rather would gladly have fled away, &c.,[1]

On the morrow, the Monday before the Assumption of the Mother of God, we again conveyed the carriage up stream on the Rhone from this place, Seseli, more than half a mile, not being able to go with the carriage any other way. Afterwards we drove through superinfernal mountains to the imperial city of Genew (Geneva). Here we arrived amidst very violent rain; and a certain rich and senseless old woman, after receiving us into the Angel Inn, drove us out

---

[1] Alluding to Psalm lv. 6, " O that I had wings like a dove, for then would I flee away and be at rest."

again from the inn into the rain, on learning that we were Bohemians, and called us heretics. Here we obtained by entreaty a reception in an inn, the fourth from that old woman's. It was not till the morrow, Tuesday, that Lord Albert and his suite arrived on horseback. Here two respectable citizens came to Lord Albert, and when Lord Albert told them, that the King of Bohemia had entered into a league or friendly relations with the King of France, on hearing that they were greatly terrified, because they have something in question with the King of France, and especially because the King of France covets them, wishing to bring them under his feudal sovereignty.

On the morrow, Wednesday, the day of the Assumption of the Mother of God, we travelled ten very long leagues, along a lake to the town of Luzan (Lausanne); and here the last Frenchman, who was to have made carpets, ran away from us. In this town they have in a church many indulgences of the Mother of God, and large numbers of people, both men and women, invoking her, and priests.

On the morrow, Thursday, we travelled three long miles, through mountains higher than in Bohemia, to a fortified town, named Modun (Moudon). Here we entered into the country of Switzerland.

On the morrow we travelled five miles to Freiburg, a very strong and well fortified Swiss city.

On the morrow, Saturday, we travelled three very long Bohemian miles to the city of Pern (Berne), which is the chief city in Switzerland, and is tolerably handsome and strong. That day on arriving we went immediately to the bath, and bathed with good-looking female citizens, damsels and dames, all together.

On the morrow, Sunday, after breakfast we travelled four long Bohemian miles to the village of Longetel, in Bohemian "Longvale."

On the morrow, Monday, we travelled five very long Bohemian miles to the city of Paden (Baden), in Switzerland, by a very bad road. On the road we breakfasted in the city of Ora (Aarau), and here there came to us a beautiful lady, a native of the country, who wondered at us beyond measure exceedingly. When we arrived at Paden, we stayed there on Tuesday and Wednesday, and bathed with good-looking damsels and ladies and countesses, and were merry; so that Lord Bavor again lamented that he had ever married. And the vicar of the Bishop of Constance, and the rest of the priesthood and monks bathed, as well as some ladies who had come with them from Constance.

On the morrow, the Thursday before St. Bartholomew, we travelled from Paden four very long miles to the city of Wintertuorn.

On the morrow, Friday, the day of St. Bartholomew (Aug. 24), we travelled four very long miles to Kostnitze (Constance), on the Rhine, where the wicked Germans burned Magister John Huss. That night, when we lay there, it thundered very violently, and almost the whole night through the priests were ringing bells to stop the thunder, especially at St. Peter's *in summo*, where they condemned Magister Huss to death.

On the morrow, Saturday, we travelled on the lake, getting into a boat, five miles to the fortified town of Pregnitz (Bregenz), on the shore of the lake; and the grooms led the horses round the lake after us. Here we stayed, and rested our horses in Pregnitz Sunday and Monday. This is already in Ecz[1] (Tyrol).

On the morrow, Tuesday, we travelled five miles in the land of Prince Sigismund of Tyrol, to a fortified town in the mountains, named Plugentz (Pludenz).

On the morrow, Wednesday, we drove four miles, or rather we all went on foot rather than drove, through the enormous Carinthian mountains to a village named Pugnen.

On the morrow, Thursday, we travelled two long miles to the village of Landek, above which is a castle belonging to the Prince.

---

[1] Ecz is the Bohemian name of the river Adige, which rises in the Tyrol.

On the morrow, Friday, we travelled six long miles to a mansion named Petenau. The mansion and inn were very well furnished, but the hostess was a very ill-natured old woman, who called us and all Bohemians, heretics.

On the morrow, Saturday (Sept. 1), we travelled three miles to the city of Ispurk (Innsbruck), where Prince Sigismund of Tyrol resides and has his court; but at that time the prince and princess had gone away on account of the plague. We stayed in a very well-furnished and excellent inn.

On the morrow, Sunday, we travelled a mile to the city of Halla, where salt is manufactured. Here we got immediately into a boat, for which we had sent Leonard, who had obtained two large boats. In one we conveyed twenty-nine horses, and went ourselves in the other, down the river Jin (Inn) as far as Pasow. That day we sailed five miles from Halla to a city belonging to Ludwig, Prince of Bavaria, named Rotenburk (Rattenburg). There is a handsome castle above the town, and obliging people in the town.

On the morrow, the Monday after St. Jilji (St. Giles), we sailed twelve miles to a city also belonging to Prince Ludwig, named Wasserburg. The city is tolerably handsome and strong, the river Inn flows round it, and there is also a castle belonging to the Prince in it.

On the morrow, Tuesday, we sailed eight long miles to the city of Praunau. That day we sailed past the city of Mildorf, which is tolerably handsome, and Etink (Oetting), which is also handsome.

On the morrow, Wednesday, we sailed eight miles to the city of Pasow (Passau), and sailed past the city of Sardink. Here in Pasow they told us, that there was great mortality in Bohemia, and that the King of Bohemia, our gracious lord, had gone with the Queen's Majesty and the princes from Prague to the city of Most on account of the plague. And Lord Albert, who had intended to ride to His Majesty with two or three others, bethought himself in consequence and would not go any where away from his suite and the carriage, and that on account of the plague. For we were all much grieved and terrified, when they told us that there was great mortality in Bohemia.

On the morrow, Thursday, we sailed seven miles down stream below Pasow on the Dunaj (Danube), to a village,[1] . . . . . . and

---

[1] Another gap due to the Austrian censorship of the press.

they led the horses round by land as far as the village.

On the morrow, Friday, we travelled from this village away from the Danube four miles, to a town belonging to Lord John of Rosenberg, named Frimburk, and here we entered Bohemia. That day we breakfasted in the town of Hazlach.

On the morrow, Saturday, the Nativity of the Virgin Mary, the Mother of God, we travelled five long miles to Bohemian Budweis. That day, half-a-mile from Krumlow, which belongs to the Lord of Rosenberg, Lord Albert Kostka became very ill, so that he barely travelled thence to the monastery of the Holy Crown. On the morrow he got better, and the abbot of the monastery took him in his own carriage to Budweis. Here in Budweis they told us that the King's Majesty, our gracious lord, was in the city of Jihlava (Iglau). The abbot took Lord Albert forthwith to the castle of Hluboka, for in Budweis also people had begun to die.[1]

On the morrow, Monday, we travelled four long miles to Jindrichow Hradetz ('Henry's castle): and here they told us, that His Royal Majesty was going to Brno (Brünn), in Moravia.

On the morrow, Tuesday, we travelled four miles to Jihlava (Iglau), and here we already heard, how one person was not expected to live, another was dead, another was ill.

On the morrow, Wednesday, Lord Albert went in the carriage with only three others to His Royal Majesty at Brünn, and sent his suite home to Litomysl. That day we only drove four miles to Meziritze in Moravia.

On the morrow, Thursday, we drove four

---

[1] *i. e.* of the plague.

miles to the town of Tishnow; and here we disguised ourselves, for we feared robbery.

On the morrow, Friday (September 14), we drove three miles to Brünn. Here we delivered our letters to His Royal Majesty and completed our embassy. To the Omnipotent Lord God be glory for it for ever and ever! Amen.

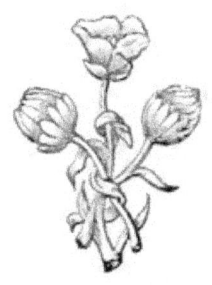

POSTSCRIPT.

IT is almost needless to add that this embassy produced no practical effect and bore no fruit. As in the council of the King of France, so also in Europe generally the ecclesiastical power was too strong for any open combination to be formed against it by secular princes, especially with an Utraquist monarch at its head. Ere long the principle that " no faith need be kept with heretics" was put in practice against King George in the most flagrant manner by his own son-in-law, Matthias Corvinus, King of Hungary. The same fraudulent ecclesiastical system that then weakened and finally ruined the noble Czeskish nation, has more lately busied itself in tampering with the documents of nations and individuals that have refused to submit to its sway, and we see its working in what has just been laid in a mutilated state before the reader. The hand of retribution appears at the present day to be overtaking it; whether finally or not, is a problem as yet beyond the power of human intelligence to solve.

A. H. Wratislaw.

www.ingramcontent.com/pod-product-compliance
Lightning Source LLC
Chambersburg PA
CBHW020323090426
42735CB00009B/1385